WALKING THE NORFOLK LONG DISTANCE TRAIL
THE COAST PATH

Further details of Poppyland Publishing titles can be found at
www.poppyland.co.uk
where clicking on the 'Support and Resources' button
will lead to pages specially compiled to support this book.

WALKING THE NORFOLK LONG DISTANCE TRAIL

The Coast Path

PHOTOGRAPHS: MIKE ROBINSON
TEXT: BRUCE ROBINSON

POPPYLAND PUBLISHING

ISBN 0 946148 77 5 / 978 0 946148 77 6

Published by Poppyland Publishing, Cromer, NR27 9AN

Designed and set in 10 on 13 pt Gilgamesh Book by Watermark, Cromer, NR27 9AL.

Printed by Printing Services (Norwich) Ltd

Page 2: **Holme beach at dusk, looking towards Gore Point.**

Foreword

Perhaps it all began when Rome introduced Britons to planned roads that ran for many miles; or perhaps the genetic seed was sown 2,000 years before, when hunters followed migrating herds along the chalk ridge from the South Coast along the Ridgeway to East Anglia.

Whatever the origin, we now seem to have a need to travel on foot for pleasure.

Twenty years ago no one really knew how many people would walk, cycle or ride the new Peddars Way and Norfolk Coast Path. It was well signed and it had a dedicated officer caring for it. Those were the halcyon days when money was easy to come by and management consisted of cutting grass and repairing the odd sign.

The 21st-century National Trail is a far cry from this.

Management is now hi-tech and completely dedicated to ensuring that walkers, cyclists and horse riders really enjoy their National Trail experience. We know who uses the route, where they come from, and why. GPS, GIS, visitor surveys, people counters, baggage carriers, business, package holidays, websites, promotion, marketing, environmental sustainability and Quality Standards are all part of the National Trail world.

So where does the National Trail of the future lead?

Twenty years from now visitor patterns and transport could have altered beyond recognition because of climate change. Indeed, the precise line of the Coast Path may be different because of sea level rise. However, we will still have the same beautiful landscape, the same flint villages and the same sense of challenge and achievement when you have walked all or part of the route.

Read this book, enjoy the wonderful images; then put your boots on and challenge yourself. One day or eight, it does not matter; just follow the footsteps of our ancestors and take up the challenge.

TIM LIDSTONE-SCOTT
Manager, Norfolk Long Distance Trail
Spring 2006

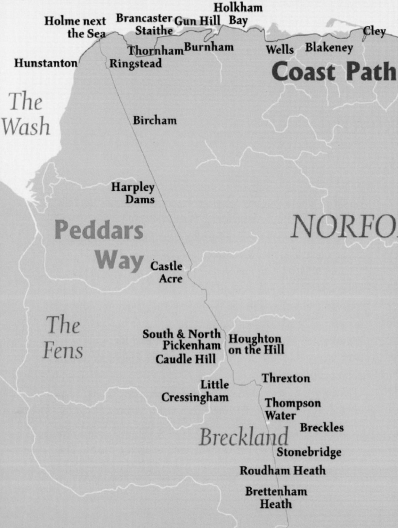

Holme next
the Sea

Brancaster
Staithe

Holkham
Bay

Gun Hill

Weybourne
Hope

Cley

Sheringham

Hunstanton

Thornham

Burnham

Wells

Blakeney

Runton

Ringstead

Roman
Camp

Cromer

Coast Path

*The
Wash*

Bircham

Harpley
Dams

The Broads

NORFOLK

**Peddars
Way**

Castle
Acre

*The
Fens*

South & North
Pickenham
Caudle Hill

Houghton
on the Hill

**The Norfolk
Long Distance Trail**

Little
Cressingham

Threxton

Thompson
Water

Breckles

Breckland

Stonebridge

Roudham Heath

Brettenham
Heath

Walking the Coast Path

One breezy day in July 1986, HRH The Prince of Wales, staff in hand, came striding over the dunes and on to the beach at Holme next the Sea to join a jubilant yet respectful crowd. Hands were shaken, introductions made and speeches delivered. Then Norfolk's official national long distance walking route — The Peddars Way and Norfolk Coast Path — was declared open. Applause mingled with the sound of the sea, and the thread of tension broke. The waiting was over, and the 93-mile route — the long awaited result of so many people's hard work — was finally in being. Slowly, the crowd broke up and an invited group, including Prince Charles and TV comedian and writer Mike Harding — then the Ramblers' Association standard bearer — began a relaxed stroll over the sands in the direction of Old Hunstanton where, for some of us, a sit-down meal awaited.

In that crowded room, amid the hubbub and between courses, table companion Mike Harding told me a joke. Twenty years on I cannot remember what it was. The joke, that is. But I do remember with great clarity that for everyone present the events of that marvellous day represented a satisfying end to a very long journey.

Twenty years on, the trail is now part and parcel of Norfolk's leisure and tourism framework, so familiar and reassuring that it is as though we have never been without it. But its cheerful birth was not achieved without a hard fight by many people over a great deal of time, for the idea of a long distance route was actually first mooted by Norfolk County Council in 1969, 17 years before the royal ceremony on the beach. This book, and its companion volume on the PeddarsWay section, therefore celebrates in words and photographs the first two decades of Norfolk's very own long distance trail.

⇐ **The Peddars Way and Coast Path. Walkers seeking detailed guidance will need Ordnance Survey Landranger maps 132, 133 and 144. More information is under 'Support and Resources' at www.poppyland.co.uk.**

The Coast Path section is unlike its national trail counterpart, the Peddars Way, in many different ways, one being that whereas the Way is an ancient route, the Coast Path is relatively new and was specially created because the Norfolk section of the Roman road, on its own, was not deemed long enough to qualify as an LDR under the Countryside Commission's rules at the time. It quickly became apparent, however, that the coastal section was a gem in its own right. Today, many people choose to walk these coastal paths in preference to the inland line of the Peddars Way. And some people use the Coast Path as a first introduction to the art and pleasures of long-distance walking. Frankly, I enjoy the contrasting delights of both sections. My interest in the Late Iron Age and Early Roman periods, sated by three or four days spent wandering along the Peddars Way, gives way to the purest of pleasure to be gained from the wide skies, seascapes and marshes encountered along the coast. Let no one say one section is better than the other. Together, they are the sum total of an altogether delightful experience.

Hunstanton was a regular youthful recreational destination, and as a teenager I spent many Sundays in summer cycling there from home in Lincolnshire. The sun, the breeze and the brightness all added to the pleasure, on a clear day, of catching a glimpse of Boston Stump on the far side of the Wash. Reaching Hunstanton from Knettishall on foot is also a confident affirmation that your walk might actually be heading for a successful completion, something which might well have seemed in doubt when, exhausted and seared by the sun on the long stretch by Anmer Minque, perhaps, doubts had crept into the mind.

Some of these coastal areas — Hunstanton, Brancaster, Salthouse, Blakeney and so on — were sorely savaged by the Great Flood of 1953, and many people lost their lives. It was an illustration not only of the power of nature but of the fragility of the coastline and the futility of efforts to protect it. Of course, the Hunstanton most visitors see is 'new' only in

9

⇐ A low sun breaks through clouds over the Wash at Hunstanton.

Summer at Hunstanton and the land train moves tourists between the sea front and the cliffs. ⇒

Razorshell sand piles at low tide, Holme beach.

A beach nest in the Holme Nature Reserve.

the sense that it was begun in 1846 by Henry le Strange and given an almighty boost by the arrival of the railway in 1862. Like Cromer, it retains something of the feel and genteel air of a late-Victorian seaside town. Alas, the railway and even the pier (destroyed by a storm in 1978) have gone, but it is still sufficiently bright and breezy to rekindle many old memories.

Our group was once washed out of its tents on a campsite in Hunstanton when, suddenly and utterly unexpectedly, a squall blew up during the night. Torrential rain lashed the camp site and flooded part of the camp ground, and we spent some of the night trying to keep warm and dry in the cold, dark and otherwise deserted campsite clubroom.

A sight of the Wash also brings forth two other recollections, both of them to do with aircraft. The first, experienced when flying from Edinburgh to Norwich, was a view from the aircraft window of the Wash inverted, as it were, with the sea at the bottom and King's Lynn at the top, the very opposite of the picture usually presented by maps. The other came in the late 1970s while being given a ride in an RAF Jaguar jet from Coltishall, when the pilot dropped down over the sea to 200 feet in order to do a simulated attack on targets at the Holbeach bombing and firing range, and when the view from the cockpit gave rise to the feeling that we were flying lower than the tops of Hunstanton cliffs. I was never so scared in my whole life.

A sea fisherman on the beach
in front of Hunstanton cliffs. ⇒

Holme Dunes

Beginning a journey nearly fifty miles inland on the edge of Suffolk, and then walking north-west and finally reaching the sea, is always a thrill. After several days of gravelled or metalled roads under your feet, the sudden transition to stiff grass and yielding sand takes a moment to comprehend. But it is no less enjoyable for that. Holme beach has a feeling of specialness about it, an atmosphere of being at the end of something, and arrival there never fails to please even if the beach itself is less picturesque and far muddier now than it used to be. Our usual walking routine has been to walk on to the beach, shake hands (because we'd actually got there), enjoy the sea air for a while and maybe paddle, if the tide was in, and then seek somewhere secluded for a rest. On the landward side of the dunes is the board-walk, and towards the eastern end of the boardwalk is a clump of pines. One year, I recall, two of us dropped our rucksacks, had a bite to eat, and then lay down to take a breather. I did not wake up until two hours later.

⇐ **The beach entrance at Holme Nature Reserve.**

The Coast Path heads towards The Firs, part of Holme Nature Reserve. *Inset:* **The boardwalk clings to the dunes behind Holme beach.** ⇒

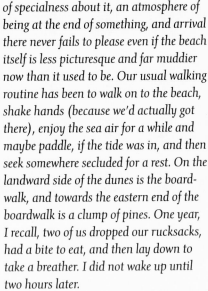

Whichever way you decide to turn, west to Hunstanton or east to Cromer — the delights of sunny Hunny, or the Lifeboat pub at Thornham — Holme is an essential part of the whole experience of walking the long distance route, not because it marks some sort of half-way point but because of the undoubted atmosphere of this wind-blown corner of the Norfolk coastline. Sometimes called Gore Point, it has a much darker look than it had once because beach erosion is taking place and the tides are busily washing away 4,000-year-old peat layers and exposing — as Norfolk Egyptologist Howard Carter once remarked, in quite another context — wonderful things.

For a number of years strollers on the beach had noticed pieces of old posts, but in 1998 a circle of ancient timbers, subsequently dubbed Seahenge, with a central upturned tree bole, was spotted and reported. Experts took a look, realised its significance, decided the timbers were at risk, and in 1999 took them away for safety reasons and for study. It caused a furore but their decision, I think, was surely justified because of the weight of additional information subsequently gained. Samples of the timbers were subjected to scientific testing, and eventually some dates emerged: 2050 BC for the up-turned oak bole and 2049 BC for the timber posts. Moreover, the timbers had been cut by Early Bronze Age axes, and they had been hauled into position, on what was then marginal land between the coast and the sea, by people using honey-suckle ropes. It was assumed the location and the construction was used for funeral rites. Then in 2004 a second circle was found. This one was discovered to be three hundred years older than the first one.

To put both of them into some sort of context, the dating is around the time that Grimes Graves flint mines were in production, a new building phase was under way at Stonehenge, and Sumerian scribes were busily writing and copying what has become known as the Epic of Gilgamesh.

The plan at the time of writing this book is that some of the Seahenge 1 and 2 timbers will be, probably and finally, placed for public display in a refurbished museum at King's Lynn. The projected date for this is 2007. Meanwhile, with constant beach and tidal movement on the coast, and erosion continuing, the feeling is that other significant discoveries on Holme beach may be around the corner, and strollers are urged to keep looking. For example, some people think that somewhere out there may have been a wharf, or at least loading and unloading facilities, at the seaward terminus of the Peddars Way. Seahenge 1 and 2 may not be the end of the story.

Clatter along the boardwalk at Brancaster Staithe Green — occasionally accompanied in front and behind by horses seeking relief from the boggy ground, or simply wishing to make new friends — and sooner or later you come across a sign on the landward side indicating the site

⇐ **The tide laps gently against Holme beach at dusk, near the sites of Seahenge 1 and 2.**

A tractor lost to the reeds at Brancaster.

⇑ A spring tide submerges the path at Burnham Deepdale.

A sailing boat near Stiffkey Greens. ⇒

⇓ Mudflats at the old Thornham staithe.

Site of the Roman quay near Branodunum Roman fort, Brancaster.

of Branodunum. Archaeology buffs and the curious might be disappointed that there is actually little to see save grass, but there is much history hereabouts. Most of the physical remains were carted away years ago to form, so it is said, the basis of many a local farm barn, while ashlar blocks, probably facing stones from the perimeter defences, were built into the south wall of Brancaster parish church as long ago as the 12th century.

Branodunum is classified as a Roman Fort of the Saxon Shore, one of a string of such constructions evidently used as defences against maurading Saxon invaders who were constantly nibbling at Rome's northern boundaries. But there seems to be more to it than that, and some experts have argued that the real picture was actually more complicated. For example, although there is no sign of an early fort at Brancaster (though there was a fort-like enclosure), there is evidence to suggest there might have been a military site here before the establishment of the Shore Fort. This, in turn, was replaced around AD 200 by another military installation a little to the south; and this was replaced about AD 225–250 by an even larger fort. To the east and west of the main fort site was a large civilian settlement. There have been numerous finds in the area, including finger rings, while other evidence suggests that cavalry of the *Cohors 1 Aquitanorum* might well have been stationed there for a time.

What was this place for? Latterly, no doubt, it was used to defend the shoreline against possible incursions. Another thought is that some of these forts, including Brancaster, were built originally as naval bases to control trade routes and merchant shipping. Perhaps this was where some of Norfolk's livestock and farm produce was shipped out, and where the tolls and taxes were collected.

To the inexperienced or the overloaded, or even to the unlucky, blisters can become a very tender subject. It was a regular topic of conversation and debate during the years of our early expeditions when techniques were primitive and our loads were heavy. Essentially, it boiled

Basking seals near Blakeney Point. ⇒

Burnham sea bank

Preparing to venture on to Burnham sea bank (or Blakeney, or Overy for that matter), particularly for the first time, is a little like planning to walk across Halvergate Marsh. You need to check your waterproofs, if not your meteorological forecasts, and glance at the sky and at the wind direction to see what sort of weather is blowing in. In other words, it's exciting. Out there, on the edge of the world, you feel vulnerable and yet elated, both at the same time. The wind tugs at your hair, the sky is huge, and in those moments you know precisely why you walk and why you enjoy it so much. This time, what draws you on is not simply a need to know what is round the next corner, but the sheer pleasure of being alive. If you are caught in driving rain, of course, priorities and philosophies change, because there is no shelter; but if you don't take the risk here, you won't take it anywhere.

down to the simple option: to burst, or not to burst. Over time I fell in line with the aforementioned school of thought, and even carried a clean pin in my rucksack precisely for that purpose, along with supplies of Elastoplast and Germolene. ('Ah, the smell of Germolene in the morning!') Over the years, techniques evolved to the point where the main object has been to avoid any blisters in the first place. Everything was geared to that. Feet were smeared with cream before socks and boots were put on in the morning; the walk was halted the moment any discomfort at all was felt, and socks were pulled straight and boots re-tied, just to shift the pressure points; while during midday stops boots and socks were taken off, feet and boots were aired, and the socks changed

Blisters and chafing — a very tender subject.

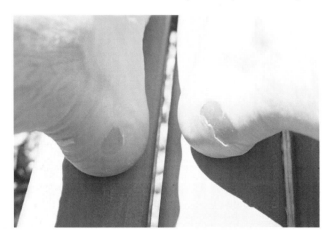

over from one foot to the other before re-lacing began. Not a completely foolproof set of techniques, though I have to say the condition of my feet while walking has not been a big problem since I started doing it.

A bracing walk along the edge of Norfolk's shoreline or salt marshes renews your zest for life. I once spent a restful and informative half-hour watching a fisherman busy among the shellfish ponds at Brancaster Staithe, and afterwards wondered where the time had gone. It is easy to pause here and listen to the wind and the incessant slap-slap of rigging on metal masts, stare at forgotten old timbers sticking forlornly out of muddy creeks, and taste and smell the sea. At the same time, it is also easy to forget just how important and busy this part of Norfolk once was. I tend to remember Blakeney for some of the best pub fish and chips in the business, or as a gentle leisure location. But Blakeney, along with its neighbours, Cley and Wiveton, once formed a Golden Triangle of maritime economic success. The sounds in those days, when the old estuary was one of the largest shipping facilities in the country, included the slap of rigging on timber mast, the shouts of chandlers and merchants and sailors, the clang of smiths and the hammer of carpenters, and the patient clop of pack trains. You can still find the graves of seamen in the churchyard at Cley.

All this is difficult to grasp unless you happen to catch

A shellfish cleansing pool near Brancaster Staithe. ⇒

a glimpse of the docks at Yarmouth, or see vessels in The Roads, plying back and forth. But there were once wharf facilities all along this coastline, and ships everywhere. If you don't believe me, turn off the trail for half an hour and stroll up the slope towards Salthouse church, and when you get there take a close look at the backs of some of the pews. Here you will see, crudely but tellingly scratched into sections of the old woodwork, pictures of medieval boats no doubt created quite illegally during particularly lengthy sermons. If you think about it, the perpetrators of these sketches might even have stood beside the church, looked down the slope, and watched these very vessels about their work.

Another indication that these were also disaster-haunted shores comes with the realisation that at the beginning of the 20th century there were 27 lifeboat stations between Hunstanton and Aldeburgh (Suffolk). Dozens of ships and thousands of men perished at sea helping to grease the wheels of land-based industry, and keeping the home fires burning. But it is the former Blakeney, Cley and Wiveton estuary which really catches the imagination. Stand beside Cley church, or on Wiveton's ancient bridge, and you can still make out the shape of the former estuary. In 1953 there were particularly severe storms and flooding along the entire eastern seaboard, and sea water flooded in again. A memorable aerial photograph was taken at the time, and for

⇐ A solitary boat sails out to open sea beyond Blakeney Point.

a few days, and until the waters subsided, the old estuary reappeared like a ghost from the past.

Cley's shingle beach can be torture for unfit or elderly walkers. The stones grind relentlessly at your leg muscles, and I have seen brave men tremble after a mere hundred yards or so. Other than a brief visit to gaze at the sea and the surf, it is a stretch of the trail I have usually avoided, preferring to take the grassy track on the landward side of the sea bank. East Bank is one of the most famous bird-watching locations in the county; some would say, in the country. Indeed, in the decades since the seamen and cargoes and the sailing ships disappeared from the estuary Cley has based its fame on birds. When I first started to haunt the area there was a quite ordinary café in the middle of the village, in what always looked like a private house, in which enthusiasts gathered to sip tea or coffee, talk about birds, and enter sightings into the daily birding diary. If the café owner was temporarily out of sight, and the phone rang, then a customer would take the call. It was invariably a birder or twitcher on some quest or other, or seeking information. 'This is John in Scotland. I'm working my way down the East Coast. Anything interesting at Cley at the moment?' I expect there usually was. The mecca for birders is now the George Hotel, where the birding bible is kept and where damp wellies and khaki waterproofs are part of the furniture and fittings. With more people joining the RSPB, and more people taking time out to look, there has been a big increase in the numbers of birdwatchers in recent years. It is usually easy to

A group of twitchers tracking birds near Weybourne cliff.

The 'birders' Bible' at the George Hotel, Cley.

spot them in their seasonal plumage: dull green waterproofs, festoons of cameras, telescopes, tripods and binoculars (called 'bins' by the regulars) and, very often, with distinctive woolly hats. A strange breed, but no real threat to walkers.

The sort of leisure walking I have indulged in over the years has not been competitive in any way, shape or form, but I do recall feeling utterly defeated on one occasion. Our group had called into the café on the beach at Cley for some relief from the chilly breeze and for a warming cup of coffee. There was only one other customer, also drinking coffee, a young chap dressed not in anorak, trousers and boots, but in singlet and shorts. The only equipment he seemed to be carrying was a small bottle of water. We got into conversation and asked what he was doing, and it was then he said he had started in Cromer that very morning and was planning to jog all the way to Knettishall. If he jogged all night, he thought, the journey would take him a day and a half. We were planning to take seven days to cover the same distance. Later, trudging towards Salthouse and still within sound of the sea, we consoled ourselves with the thought that we were completing the route deliberately slowly in order to soak in the sights and experiences, whereas he would be able to appreciate very little. That was our reasoning, anyway.

The Salthouse shingle bank stretches for about four miles from Cley beach to Weybourne Hope. ⇒

Gun Hill & Holkham

Parts of the Battle Area notwithstanding, I cannot think of any finer view in Norfolk than that which reveals itself as you reach the summit of the sandy dunes at Gun Hill to be confronted by the spectacular sky-filling vastness of Holkham Bay. On a clear, sunny day it is an exquisite vista, sea and sand framed by a vast blue arc and by curving tree-fringed dunes.

Let us be truthful. It can sometimes induce other feelings. Unless you seek out a seam of drying sand it is sometimes difficult to find a firm, comfortable footing. Too wet, and the salt turns your walking boots speckled white overnight. Too dry, and your boots fill with sand as they sink in up to the ankles.

Our group once had to seek shelter in a narrow sand pocket as a gale-force wind, howling from the direction of Hunstanton and the polar regions, scoured across the Bay and sent razor-sharp clouds of sand bowling across the beach. On another occasion, so penetrating was the heat brought on by the sun beating down on sand we had to retreat to the trees to seek shade from the blistering, windless atmosphere.

But these were exceptions. Holkham is Holkham, which means it is one of the finest vistas in the whole of Norfolk, and one of the main reasons why the Coast Path is such a very special route indeed.

Holkham Bay viewed from the dunes near Gun Hill. ⇒

⇐ **The tide rolls back in to reclaim Holkham Beach.**

Today, it is genuinely difficult to imagine Norfolk without its LDR, for the paths have stitched themselves seamlessly into the fabric of the area. Usage is another matter, and it has to be admitted that it is is not the most heavily used of the long distance routes. As in most things, however, it may be yet another example of Norfolk doing different because the trail has a very individual appeal. The two paths (the Peddars Way and the Coast Path, and particularly the latter) are used a lot, particularly at weekends by casual users needing a breath of fresh air or wanting to take the dog for a walk. Carriers of rucksacks intent on walking the entire distance

Birdwatchers by the old Thornham staithe.

The view across Brancaster bay and the Titchwell Nature Reserve. In the far distance are the pinewoods behind Holkham beach.

— which can be as much as 96 miles if you take in Hunstanton — have a lower profile. There are a couple of points to be made. One is that because there are no notoriously strenuous sections, and because the route is classified as being of 'moderate' difficulty, it does not have much appeal to 50-mile a day yompers who want to test themselves to the limit. They tend to head for greater heights and bigger obstacles. On the other hand, it does appeal to older walkers and those wanting to tackle a long distance route perhaps for the first time, a majority spending between eight and 14 days on the trail.

A user survey of 1995/96 helped define the concepts of short and long distance users who, between them, accounted for something like 103,000 user days on the trail. More interestingly still, there were some 80,000 of them who together injected something like £1,500,000 into the local economy. None of this suggests under-use, but it would be nice to think that even more youngsters, particularly, might experience it in the future, for among other things the path does have a role as a teaching tool. History weighs heavily on each and every one of its miles. And aside from history

Wells

Wells is a heady cultural mix of commercial (or seaborne) and tourist interests, much as Sheringham used to be, and it still seems to be able to combine dock work with bingo halls and cargoes with caravans and camp sites, with no sign of a split personality. I like the place. The two faces of the town compete with each other and jostle for attention, and there is a sort of 'take me as I am' feeling that suggests, perhaps, it has got the mix just about right. Much of the old work of the docks has also evaporated, but they are still busy, still gritty, and still manage to combine business and fun with the healthy smell of the sea. It is also a rather good place to replenish the rucksack as you prepare for the final stretch to Cromer and the end of the route.

Swans gather to feed at Wells quay. ⇒

Turning the train ready for the return trip to Wells on the narrow gauge railway. ⇓

Windsurfing at dusk in front of West Sands at Wells.

⇑ A couple enjoying the sunset at Wells beach.

High tide pulls gently on the moorings of a rowing boat in the entrance to Wells quay. ⇒

and botany, bird-watching and fresh air, it also reveals to the receptive mind a continuously changing landscape: breck, chalk, forest, mid-county, high county, agriculture and tourism, cliff and coast, salt marsh, shoreline, seaside and so on. There is also a useful walking holiday strand, too. Mind you, the joy of the route for me has always been its gentleness, its peace and its openness.

Incidentally, at the time of writing yet another User Survey is in the process of being organised in the hope that these new results will also aid management planning for the trail for the next 20 years. The survey should also indicate how communities and businesses along the route can be supported and encouraged, and help build an even more detailed picture of the users themselves.

Camping along the Coast Path — which is more built up, heavily populated and more proprietorial than the Peddars Way — usually means organised, established camp sites. They are an acquired taste. The alternative is yet another acquired taste: landladies, and bed and breakfast establishments. I confess that once one reaches the years of maturity then there is something comfortable and comforting about the prospect of a shower and a proper bed at the end of a tiring day, and most of those I have tried I would place in categories between OK and Excellent. Using B&Bs for a week

The Long Distance Route runs along the edge of the salt marshes at Warham Green. ⇒

Unloading the catch on Weybourne beach.

on the LDR does, it has to be admitted, push up the cost. On the other hand, they have an obvious advantage and an obvious allure when the alternative is struggling to cook a meal or erect a tent in a hedge bottom on a rainy night. Without exception, the landladies I have met have happily and sympathetically coped with dripping waterproofs, damp clothes and muddy boots. And offered English fried breakfasts.

One lovely lady in Sedgeford, seeing our reluctance to leave in the morning because of a hard rain falling, apologised because she had to go off to work. So she left us to finish our breakfasts, gave us the house key, suggested we read the newspapers and wait until the rain stopped, and merely asked us to lock up when we left and pop the key through the letterbox. We accepted her plan with gratitude.

They used to say of Weybourne Hope, or Hoop, that it was the most defended area in England. True or not, its deep waters and shelving beach, which allow for the possibility of deep-draught boats anchoring close in to the shore, has provoked military interest at least since the days of Elizabeth I. This is the one place, strategists have thought, where invasion fleets could send ashore their invading hordes. In consequence, it has a very long history of association with the military, even with Queen Elizabeth I herself, for it was she first who ordered elaborate defences to be erected, on this occasion against the Spanish. Throughout both 20th

Golden cliffs rise out of the shingle at Weybourne. ⇒

The wireless station at Kelling Hard.

century world wars troops were stationed here, coastal guns were in position, and military entanglements and concrete constructions littered the low beaches and cliff tops. Even during the Cold War, radar detection equipment, our front line defence against low-flying enemy aircraft, was stationed hereabouts. Indeed, if you search long enough you

A relic of the second world war at Weybourne.

Keeping vigil: Sheringham Coast Watch Lookout Station.

One of the North Norfolk Railway's Poppy Line steam trains prepares to leave Weybourne station.

The view west towards Sheringham from the top of Beeston Bump.

The view from Beeston Bump towards West Runton.

Roman Camp

When the children were young and the world was not so old we used to drive to Roman Camp to erect our tent for a few days' camping or, as the family grew up, to see the bluebells and let the youngsters off the leash for a while before we had a picnic or bought ice creams at the shop. There was little or no danger on the slopes and gullies under the trees, and a great deal to be gained. A place of magic, without doubt. Sun filtering through the leaves and branches, shady glades, secret places amid the hills and hollows, and occasional glimpses of the sea. Actually, the place seems to have had very little to do with the Romans. Some of the pits and hollows are thought to have been the remains of Saxon or even Norman iron smelting operations, but the term 'Roman' was often applied to any earthwork of doubtful origin. The name will have done no harm to the cabmen from Cromer and Sheringham who took visitors for horse-drawn rides; they may have thought the name Roman Camp sounded more evocative and intriguing than Runton Heath. In the 1920s they were also able to tap into a topical public interest story, for the Romano-British town at Caistor St Edmund (*Venta Icenorum*) had just been discovered, and was the talk of the nation. No matter, Roman Camp remains a peaceful, sylvan glade.

⇐ **Sunset over West Runton beach.**

will find that the debris of war litters the area still. It was also here in 1858, incidentally, that an undersea cable was laid to Borkum in Germany, while in 1950 a cable link with Esbjerg in Denmark was established. Diplomatic exchanges evidently flowed constantly through both of them.

There is no doubt that the cliffs around East and West Runton, and some eroding dunes, are helping to rewrite British history books. When I came to write the text for the Countryside Commission's first guidebook for this route, I remember noting that the earliest evidence of people living and moving around in what we now call Britain was dated to about 400,000 years ago. Twenty years later, evidence is emerging that people were here at least 300,000 years earlier than that.

The reason is a geological phenomenon known as the Cromer Forest Bed, which outcrops at various places between the Runtons (Norfolk) and Pakefield (Suffolk). The Bed is the visible, datable remains of former river and stream systems and landscapes which existed before the last Ice Age. One branch of this ancient waterway system once departed our area in the vicinity of Cromer and West Runton, and it is these layers which tidal scouring is now exposing. There have been many fossil finds including the famous West Runton elephant, or mammoth. More recently, worked flints have been discovered which demonstrate quite clearly that 700,000 years ago hunter groups were living and navigating their way across

⇐ **West Runton beach, sea defences and cliffs.**

what is now the English Channel and parts of the North Sea.

Until about 6400 BC Britain was still joined to the Continent, the area between us and the mainland being a boggy landscape of forest, swamp and freshwater pools. Bits of this ancient forest can still be picked up on the beaches of North Norfolk, particularly around Titchwell. However, as the melt continued and sea levels rose the low-lying land bridge slowly succumbed, and Britain eventually became an island.

My father was a regular walker in that he walked to work every morning – a mile, if not a shade more – and came back for lunch; returned after lunch and came home for afternoon tea; then returned to work and came home at about 5.30 p.m. That is a grand total of about six miles a day, which he did for at least five days a week for something like 37 years. Then he went part-time. This gives an overall figure of something approaching 12,000 miles, though the real figure may well have been much higher. One of my regrets is that I have never kept a walk diary, which means I have no idea of the amount of walking I have done. It is very little compared to some who started earlier, finished later, and displayed a higher level of fitness than I was ever able to muster. On the other hand, looking back, it seems rather a lot to me.

For example, I reckon I have walked the Peddars Way at least a dozen times, completed the entire long distance route four times, and walked the circular round-Norfolk route (including Weavers Way and the Angles Way) twice, though not, I should add, as a continuous tramp.

So what would I say to anyone thinking of trying the LDR for the first time? Well, six or seven days is a handy block of time to allocate for the job, depending on your fitness levels and how much time you want to spend sightseeing. And early June is a good time to go, because the spring chill has gone, the early summer greenery is fresh and clean, and the holiday crowds have not yet arrived. This can be particularly important along the Coast Path where places like Blakeney and Sheringham sometimes sag under the weight of visitors. It also means that if bed and breakfast accommodation is being considered then it is best to book in good time. Few B&Bs, incidentally, can supply single rooms, so be prepared for twin-bedded rooms.

As for the actual walking, the first rule is to try to prevent fatigue setting in by stopping and resting *before* you get tired. Design each day as a series of, say, hour-long walks with ten-minute rests between. Walk at your own comfortable pace and do not try to adopt someone else's stride pattern. Pamper your feet by dealing with any sore place as soon as you feel it. Have a good breakfast, a very light snack lunch, and another main meal in the evening. And remember to make a good, early start, because I have always found that miles walked before midday are worth more than those walked later. Something else to remember, too, is that boots, rucksacks and legs become inexplicably heavier as the day

⇐ **The Henry Ramey Upcher lifeboat museum, Sheringham.**

wears on, so stiles, for example, gradually become higher and more difficult to climb. The difference between a 10 a.m. stile and a 4 p.m. stile can sometimes be measured in minutes.

Many changes have been noticeable on the trail over the last 20+ years. For one thing, the grass is cut regularly and obstructions are removed. But the changes have been more profound than that, reflecting changing habits, priorities, interests, attitudes and buying patterns.

Trail bikes, walking poles, hand-held GPS systems, lightweight tents, joggers, set-aside land and concessionary paths, oldie walkers and dog walkers, charity walkers and Venture Scouts, boardwalks and bridges, information boards, mobile phones and marketing strategies, holiday packages and crisp packets, bed & breakfast establishments and a much more welcoming atmosphere for walkers, web sites and metal detectors (I once saw signs of someone having attempted a little tentative prodding and scratching, though this was some time ago), guidebooks and maps. There was even, once upon a time, a line of so-called 'Romany' holiday trailers evidently disused and abandoned along the verge — now all gone, thank goodness. Despite all this, it is surprising to learn that since the official opening in 1986 there have been only two local National Trail managers overseeing it all, Michael Stagg (1986 to 1996/97) and Tim Lidstone-Scott (to present). Of course, even they had helpers, and these good folk have included: Sarah Price (National Trail assistant,

1996 to 2000), Patrick Saunders (NT works co-ordination officer, 2000 to present), Helen Levy (Objective 2 project assistant, 2005 to present), and Steve Tutt (technical assistant, 1994 to present). The paths would not be the same without them.

A few years ago two of us, having completed the 93-mile walk all the way from Knettishall, found ourselves in Cromer with time to kill on the windiest, roughest and most blisteringly cold day imaginable. The arrival of the relief column to take us home was over two hours away, most of the town was shut, and the streets were simply funnels for a scouring wind. In the end we managed to locate one small café which was still open and willing to ply us with warm cups of instant coffee until the rescue vehicle arrived. It is not the best image of the town, nor the way I really want to remember it, for Cromer also holds a particular place in my family's history.

Its heyday was the first three decades of the 20th century, but the industry that ultimately evolved into Poppyland actually began somewhat earlier, even before rail services connecting the resort with London and the Midlands arrived. The rough-hewn fishing village already had a reputation among sections of society as a gathering place for bracing bathing and therapeutic walks. But it was the railway that put icing on to the cake. In 1883 a London theatre critic of the *Daily Telegraph*, Clement Scott, wrote enthusiastically in his

⇐ **Lifeboat crew seagoing kit at Cromer lifeboat station.**

Cromer pier at dusk.

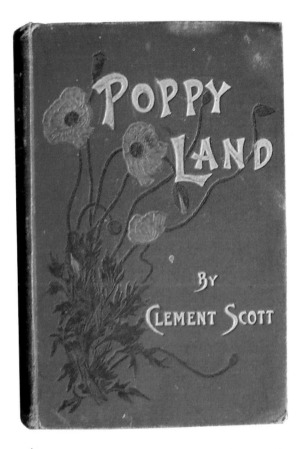

⇑ Clement Scott's articles, republished in book form.

The view out to sea from Cromer sea front. ⇒

newspaper of the quiet and colourful virtues of the area and this, in turn, also helped nudge Cromer, and Overstrand, towards a certain notoriety as the gathering place of writers and poets, politicians and the rich.

Inevitably, thanks to the railway and the low cost of fares, ordinary members of the public began to flock here, lured by the open spaces, the wind, the sea, the lighthouse, the cliffs, the fishing boats, the quaintness of the place, and by the knowledge that if Society went there then They wanted to go there, too. Inevitably, a leisure industry grew rapidly to cater for the influx. Hotels and restaurants appeared along with beach huts, deck chairs, a pier and a theatre. Even the life-boatmen became national heroes. And slowly, Cromer settled into the rhythms of serving the needs of the trippers who swarmed off the trains and flooded the beaches, and the rich, who built their big houses nearby or stayed in the hotels.

By 1926, when my parents spent their honeymoon there in a hotel overlooking the pier and the sea, Cromer was still doing the business, trading on its cosy Englishness; by 1937, however, by which time our family had doubled in size, the emphasis of the resort had shifted from Society and the rich to small hotels, lodgings, and the innocent joys of oompah and banjo bands, Pierrot shows, crabs and sandcastles, fishing boats on the beach, and strolls along the cliffs to enjoy the wind, the views, and the poppies. Family legend also says that, as a baby on a fortnight's holiday, I was bedded down at the digs each night in an open cupboard drawer.

Blissful days indeed. All of them.

Index